Pat Tillman - A Hero of War

By Philip Martin McCaulay

(DEPT OF DEFENSE/NFL/AP)

Pat Tillman – A Hero of War

Published in Raleigh, North Carolina, USA
978-0-557-19872-6

Preface

Patrick Daniel Tillman (November 6, 1976 – April 22, 2004) was an American football player who left his professional sports career and enlisted in the United States Army in 2002 in the aftermath of the September 11 attacks. He joined the United States Army Rangers and served multiple tours in combat before he was killed by friendly fire in the mountains of Afghanistan. Details about the circumstances surrounding his death have been the subject of controversy and military investigations. Pat's family and friends started the Pat Tillman Foundation to carry forward his legacy by giving students the tools and support to reach their fullest potential as leaders, no matter how they choose to serve.

Table of Contents

College Career

Pat Tillman was born on November 6, 1976 in San Jose, California; the oldest of three boys. He started his college career as a linebacker for Arizona State University in 1994, when he secured the last remaining scholarship for the team.

Tillman excelled as a linebacker at Arizona State, despite being relatively small for the position at five-feet eleven-inches (1.80 m) tall. He was named to the All-Pac-10 team three times.

As a senior in 1997, he led the Sun Devils to the Rose Bowl after an undefeated season and was voted the Pac-10 Defensive Player of the Year. Academically, Tillman graduated Summa Cum Laude with a B.S. in Marketing in three and a half years with a 3.84 GPA, and was awarded the NCAA's Post-Graduate Scholarship for academic and athletic excellence.

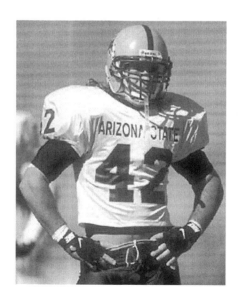

Pro Football Career

In the 1998 NFL Draft, Tillman was selected as the 226th pick by the Arizona Cardinals. Tillman moved over to play the safety position in the NFL and started ten of sixteen games in his rookie season.

Tillman broke the franchise record for tackles in 2000, and Sports Illustrated football writer Paul Zimmerman (Dr. Z) named Tillman to his NFL All-Pro team after Tillman finished with 155 tackles (120 solo), 1.5 sacks, 2 forced fumbles, 2 fumble recoveries, 9 pass deflections and 1 interception for 30 yards.

At one point in his NFL career, Tillman turned down a five-year, $9 million contract offer from the St. Louis Rams out of loyalty to the Cardinals.

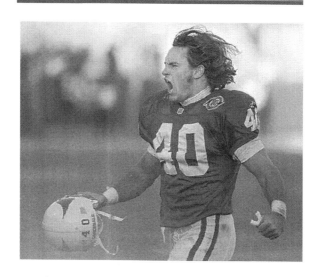

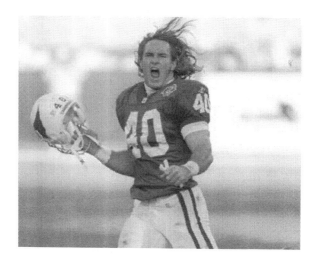

In the off-season, he competed in marathons and triathlons, while pursuing a Master's degree in history from Arizona State. He volunteered with the Boys and Girls Club of Arizona, Boys Hope Girls Hope, and the March of Dimes, and read and talked to students in schools across the Phoenix Valley.

AP photo by Brian Fitzgerald

Tillman finished his career with totals of 238 tackles, 2.5 sacks, 3 interceptions for 37 yards, 3 forced fumbles, 2 pass deflections, and 3 fumble recoveries in 60 career games. In addition he also had 1 rush attempt for 4 yards and returned 3 kickoffs for 33 yards.

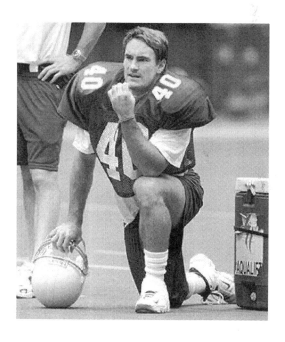

Military Career

The day after the attacks of September 11, 2001, Tillman told a reporter, "At times like this you stop and think about just how good we have it, what kind of system we live in, and the freedoms we are allowed. A lot of my family has gone and fought in wars and I really haven't done a damn thing."

He married Marie in the spring of 2002, and after returning from their honeymoon, he told the Cardinals he was going to place his NFL career on hold to become a U.S. Army Ranger with his brother, Kevin.

In May 2002, eight months after the September 11, 2001, attacks and after completing the fifteen remaining games of the 2001 season which followed the attacks (at a salary of $512,000 per year), Tillman turned down a contract offer of $3.6 million over three years from the Cardinals to enlist in the U.S. Army.

In her commentary in the June 2, 2002 Chicago Tribune, award-winning journalist Melissa Isaacson provided insight on the news of Tillman's enlistment:

> *"Tillman is the Arizona cardinal who last week told his team thanks, but he was walking away from pro football and a multi-year, multi-million dollar contract offer to join the army Rangers, elite soldiers who throughout U.S. history have specialized in dangerous missions and a force that is currently playing a major role in Afghanistan.*
>
> *At 26, Tillman said he was joining because he was approaching the Rangers' age limit of 28. He told this to his agent and his coaches and the general manager of the Cardinals, the people he had to tell.*
>
> *He did not grant interviews or answer calls. Not because he hates talking or hates sportswriters, but because Tillman and his younger brother Kevin, a minor-league baseball player who also wants to join the Rangers, do not believe they merit any special consideration or attention."*

In June 2002, Secretary of Defense Donald Rumsfeld stated "this fellow, Pat Tillman, sounds like a world-class American. We're lucky to have him."

In July 2002, he enlisted for a three-year
term, along with his brother Kevin, who
gave up the chance of a career in
professional baseball. The two brothers
completed the Ranger Indoctrination
Program in late 2002 and were assigned to
the second battalion of the 75th Ranger
Regiment in Fort Lewis, Washington.

He resided in University Place with his wife
before being deployed to Iraq.

After participating in the initial invasion of
Operation Iraqi Freedom in 2003, he
graduated from Ranger School. The Tillman
brothers were recipients of the Arthur Ashe
Courage Award at the 11th Annual ESPY
Awards in 2003.

The brothers served in Afghanistan during Operation Enduring Freedom in 2004.

Tragic Death

On the evening of April 22, 2004, Pat Tillman's unit traveled through the rugged, canyon terrain of eastern Afghanistan, and ran into an ambush. Tillman was tragically killed trying to provide cover for his fellow soldiers as they escaped from the canyon.

The Investigation

Tillman was killed in a friendly fire incident while on patrol. The specific details of his death and its aftermath were investigated by the US Congress.

The Army initially claimed that Tillman and his unit were attacked in an apparent ambush on a road outside of the village of Sperah about 25 miles (40 km) southwest of Khost, near the Pakistan border. An Afghan militia soldier was killed, and two other Rangers were injured as well.

The Army Special Operations Command initially claimed that there was an exchange with hostile forces. After a lengthy investigation conducted by Brigadier General Jones, the U.S. Department of Defense concluded that both the Afghan militia soldier's and Pat Tillman's deaths were due to friendly fire aggravated by the intensity of the firefight.

A more thorough investigation concluded that no hostile forces were involved in the firefight and that two allied groups fired on each other in confusion after a nearby explosive device was detonated.

On July 17, 2008 the United States House of Representatives Committee on Oversight and Government Reform released a report titled "Misleading Information from the Battlefield: The Tillman and Lynch Episodes".

The committee stated that its "investigation was frustrated by a near universal lack of recall" among "senior officials at the White House" and the military. It concluded:

> *"The pervasive lack of recollection and absence of specific information makes it impossible for the Committee to assign responsibility for the misinformation in Corporal Tillman's and Private Lynch's cases. It is clear, however, that the Defense Department did not meet its most basic obligations in sharing accurate information with the families and with the American public."*

Opening Statement of Rep. Henry A. Waxman
Chairman, Committee on Oversight and Government Reform
Business Meeting on Tillman Report
July 17, 2008

In April 2007, our Committee began an investigation into misleading accounts from the battlefield involving two of the most famous soldiers in Iraq and Afghanistan: Corporal Patrick Tillman, who was killed in Afghanistan on April 22, 2004, and Private Jessica Lynch, who was captured and rescued in Iraq in March and April 2003.

At our first hearing last April, we heard testimony from Kevin Tillman, a former Army Ranger, who was serving in Afghanistan with his brother, Patrick Tillman, when he was killed. For more than a month, the Tillman family and the American public were told that Pat Tillman had been killed in a valiant firefight with the enemy. President Bush praised Corporal Tillman's military service, and Corporal Tillman's patriotic memorial service was nationally televised.

Kevin Tillman told us that this account was "utter fiction." His brother was actually killed by friendly fire and Defense Department officials knew almost immediately. But they didn't tell his family, and they didn't tell the American public.

Kevin Tillman testified that he believed the Bush Administration spread this false story to garner support for the war. Here's what he told us:

In the days leading up to Pat's memorial service, media accounts, based on information provided by the Army and the White House, were wreathed in a patriotic glow and became more dramatic in tone. A terrible tragedy that might have further undermined support for the war in Iraq was transformed into an inspirational message that served instead to support the nation's foreign policy wars in Iraq and Afghanistan.

We also heard testimony from Jessica Lynch, who was captured and rescued during the opening days of the Iraq war in 2003. After Administration officials spread a false story that she bravely fought off her captors, she became a national phenomenon as "the little girl Rambo from the hills of West Virginia who went down fighting."

But that story wasn't true either. Ms. Lynch testified:

I'm still confused as to why they chose to lie and try to make me a legend. … The bottom line is the American people are capable of determining their own ideals for heroes, and they don't need to be told elaborate lies.

Both Kevin Tillman and Ms. Lynch made the same allegation: that the Administration misled the nation about their conduct in battle in order to build support for the war.

The Committee's investigation attempted to determine how this happened and who was responsible. We did not focus down the chain of command, as previous investigations had done, but instead looked up the chain of command to determine what top officials at the White House and Defense Department knew about these events, when they knew it, and what they did with their knowledge.

The Committee conducted its investigation in a bipartisan manner. The Committee reviewed tens of thousands of pages produced by the White House and the Defense Department, and we conducted more than 20 interviews with top White House and Pentagon officials.

The report before us today sets forth the results of our investigation and our conclusions.

The report begins with a premise that every member of this Committee should agree with: our nation has an inviolate obligation to share truthful information with a soldier's family and the American people should injury or death occur.

The report finds that the Administration violated this obligation. Neither the Tillman nor Lynch cases involved acts of omission. The misinformation was not caused by overlooking or misunderstanding the facts. In both cases, affirmative acts created new facts that were false.

In the days following Corporal Tillman's death, one Army official stated, "The Ranger Tillman story has been extremely positive in all media."

Another Army official said that Jessica Lynch's capture and rescue was an "awesome story."

At the White House, aides rushed to release a presidential statement before confirming whether Corporal Tillman's family had been notified. The President's top communications official, Dan Bartlett, said the story of Pat Tillman "made the American people feel good about our country … and our military."

Within days, the chief White House speechwriter, Michael Gerson, was urging his staff to collect the "most moving stuff" on Corporal Tillman for a speech by President Bush.

The report we will vote on today leaves important questions unresolved. It does not answer the fundamental question Kevin Tillman and Ms. Lynch raised at our hearing: Who was responsible for spreading these false stories?

2

That is because we encountered a striking and near uniform lack of recollection, what the *New York Times* yesterday called a widespread and self-induced case of amnesia.

In Private Lynch's case, Jim Wilkinson, the Director for Strategic Communications for CENTCOM, told the Committee he did not know where the false information originated or who disseminated it.

And in Corporal Tillman's case, even after seven Defense Department investigations, no one has been able to identify the person who created the false information about enemy fire.

Our report finds that White House officials sent or received nearly 200 e-mails concerning Corporal Tillman in the days following his death. But the White House could not produce a single e-mail or document relating to any discussion about Corporal Tillman's death by friendly fire.

Not a single written communication about personal reactions to the fratricide or the substantive, political, and public relations implications of the new information was provided to the Committee.

When White House officials thought Corporal Tillman had been killed by the enemy, the President celebrated his service. But when it came to talking about how he really died, the White House had literally nothing to say. Celebration turned to silence.

As we state in the report, if what the Committee received is accurate and complete, then the intense interest that initially characterized the White House and Defense Department's reaction to Corporal Tillman's death was followed by a stunning lack of curiosity about emerging reports of fratricide and an incomprehensible carelessness and incompetence in handling this sensitive information.

"I don't recall" is an easy response to give when you are being interviewed by congressional investigators. But the Tillman family, Ms. Lynch, and the families of all the men and women who serve in our military deserve better than "I don't recall."

I urge adoption of this report.

3

One of a Kind

The May 10, 2004 issue of *People* magazine carried a story about Pat Tillman:

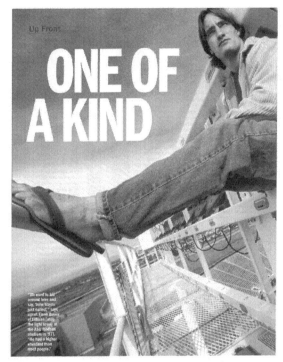

"The way the Pentagon announced the news—a simple headline: "Army Ranger Killed in Afghanistan"—is probably the way Pat Tillman would have wanted it. When Tillman, 27, walked away from a lucrative NFL career to join the Army's elite Rangers two years ago, he did so as a gesture of post-9/11 patriotism. He gave no interviews, posed for no pictures, passionately avoided publicity—and made headlines anyway. After he enlisted, his name faded from the news, and he became what he wanted to be: a soldier like hundreds of thousands of others, on active duty, trying to make whatever difference one soldier could make.

And so it was that his death in an Afghanistan fire-fight on April 22 touched so many people so deeply. Posthumously promoted to corporal, Tillman was nominated for a Bronze Star."

Two books about Tillman were recently published. Jon Krakauer, best-selling author of Into Thin Air and Into the Wild, chronicles Tillman's story in Where Men Win Glory: The Odyssey of Pat Tillman, published by Doubleday on September 15, 2009. Meanwhile, Tillman's mother, Mary Tillman, also wrote a book about her son, Boots on the Ground by Dusk, which was published on April 29, 2008.

Boots on the Ground by Dusk

Pat Tillman's mother published a book in 2008 as a tribute to her son.

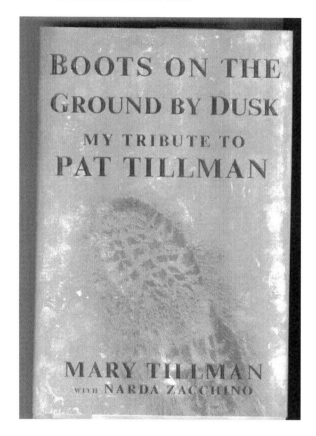

The book Boots on the Ground by Dusk has the following product description on Amazon:

"On April 22, 2004, Lieutenant David Uthlaut received orders from Khost, Afghanistan, that his platoon was to leave the town of Magarah and "have boots on the ground before dark" in Manah, a small village on the border of Pakistan. It was an order the young lieutenant protested vehemently, but the commanders at the Tactical Command Center disregarded his objections. Uthlaut split his platoon into two serials, with serial one traveling northwest to Manah and serial two towing a broken Humvee north toward the Khost highway. By nightfall, Uthlaut and his radio operator were seriously wounded, and an Afghan militia soldier and a U.S. soldier were dead. The American soldier was my son, Pat Tillman.

The Tillman family was originally informed that Pat, who had given up a professional football career to serve his country, had been shot in the head while getting out of a vehicle. At his memorial service twelve days later, they were told that he was killed while running up a hill in pursuit of the enemy. He was awarded a Silver Star for his courageous actions. A month and two days after his death, the family learned that Pat had been shot three times in the head by his own troops in a "friendly fire" incident. Seven months after Pat's death, the Tillmans requested an investigation.

Boots on the Ground by Dusk is a chronicle of their efforts to ascertain the true circumstances of Pat's death and the reasons why the Army gave the family and the public a false story. Woven into the account are valuable and respectful memories of Pat Tillman as a son, brother, husband, friend, and teammate, in the hope that the reader will better comprehend what is really lost when our sons and daughters are killed or maimed in war.

In the course of three and a half years, there have been six investigations, several inquiries, and two Congressional hearings. The Tillmans are still awaiting an outcome."

The book was reviewed favorably by David Pitt of Booklist:

"This story has made headlines for the last several years, and while there are no final answers here, those who have followed the controversy will be eager to hear from Tillman's mother."

Where Men Win Glory

In September 2009, best-selling author Jon
Krakauer published a book about Tillman.

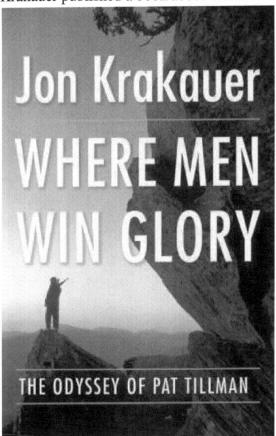

The book Where Men Win Glory has the following product description on Amazon:

"The bestselling author of Into the Wild, Into Thin Air, and Under the Banner of Heaven delivers a stunning, eloquent account of a remarkable young man's haunting journey.

Like the men whose epic stories Jon Krakauer has told in his previous bestsellers, Pat Tillman was an irrepressible individualist and iconoclast. In May 2002, Tillman walked away from his $3.6 million NFL contract to enlist in the United States Army. He was deeply troubled by 9/11, and he felt a strong moral obligation to join the fight against al-Qaeda and the Taliban. Two years later, he died on a desolate hillside in southeastern Afghanistan.

Though obvious to most of the two dozen soldiers on the scene that a ranger in Tillman's own platoon had fired the fatal shots, the Army aggressively maneuvered to keep this information from Tillman's wife, other family members, and the American public for five weeks following his death. During this time, President Bush repeatedly invoked Tillman's name to promote his administration's foreign policy. Long after

Tillman's nationally televised memorial service, the Army grudgingly notified his closest relatives that he had "probably" been killed by friendly fire while it continued to dissemble about the details of his death and who was responsible.

In Where Men Win Glory, Jon Krakauer draws on Tillman's journals and letters, interviews with his wife and friends, conversations with the soldiers who served alongside him, and extensive research on the ground in Afghanistan to render an intricate mosaic of this driven, complex, and uncommonly compelling figure as well as the definitive account of the events and actions that led to his death. Before he enlisted in the army, Tillman was familiar to sports aficionados as an undersized, overachieving Arizona Cardinals safety whose virtuosity in the defensive backfield was spellbinding. With his shoulder-length hair, outspoken views, and boundless intellectual curiosity, Tillman was considered a maverick. America was fascinated when he traded the bright lights and riches of the NFL for boot camp and a buzz cut. Sent first to Iraq—a war he would openly declare was "illegal as hell" —and eventually to Afghanistan, Tillman was driven by complicated, emotionally charged, sometimes contradictory notions of duty, honor, justice, patriotism, and masculine pride, and he was determined to serve his entire three-year commitment. But on April 22, 2004, his life would end in a barrage of bullets fired by his fellow soldiers.

Krakauer chronicles Tillman's riveting, tragic odyssey in engrossing detail highlighting his remarkable character and personality while closely examining the murky, heartbreaking circumstances of his death. Infused with the power and authenticity readers have come to expect from Krakauer's storytelling, Where Men Win Glory exposes shattering truths about men and war."

Legacy

After his death, the Pat Tillman Foundation was established to carry forward its view of Tillman's legacy by inspiring and supporting those striving for positive change in themselves and the world around them. On their website, the Pat Tillman Foundation states:

"While the story of Pat's death may have been the most publicized in the War on Terror, sadly, it is merely one of the thousands of tragic stories that deserve recognition. Pat's family and friends started the Pat Tillman Foundation to carry forward his legacy by giving students the tools and support to reach their fullest potential as leaders, no matter how they choose to serve."

The Cardinals retired his number 40, and Arizona State did the same for the number 42 he wore with the Sun Devils. The Cardinals have named the plaza surrounding their University of Phoenix Stadium in Glendale, Pat Tillman Freedom Plaza. Later, on November 12, 2006, during a Cardinals game versus the Cowboys, a bronze statue was revealed in his honor. ASU also named the entryway to Sun Devil Stadium the "Pat Tillman Memorial Tunnel" and made a "PT-42" patch that they placed on the neck of their uniforms a permanent feature.

A highway bypass around the Hoover Dam has a bridge bearing Tillman's name. The Mike O'Callaghan-Pat Tillman Memorial Bridge spans the Colorado River between Nevada and Arizona.

Lincoln Law School of San Jose has established the Pat Tillman Scholarship in honor of Tillman. Tillman's father, Patrick Kevin Tillman, earned his Juris Doctor from Lincoln in 1983.

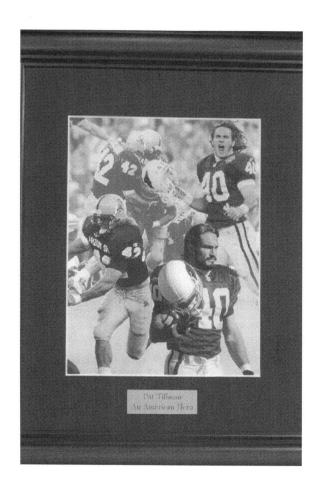

On Sunday, September 19, 2004, all teams of the NFL wore a memorial decal on their helmets in honor of Pat Tillman. The Arizona Cardinals continued to wear this decal throughout the 2004 season. Former Cardinals quarterback Jake Plummer requested to also wear the decal for the entire season but the NFL turned him down saying his helmet would not be uniform with the rest of the Denver Broncos. Plummer would later grow a full beard and his hair long in honor of Tillman, who had such a style in the NFL before cutting his hair and shaving his beard off to fit military uniform guidelines. Plummer, now retired from the NFL, has since gone back to cutting his hair short but maintains the beard.

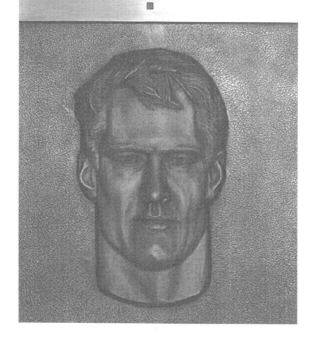

A memorial to Pat Tillman was created at Sun Devil Stadium, where he played football for the Sun Devils and the Cardinals.

Pat Tillman's high school, Leland High School in San Jose, California, renamed its football field after him.

In 2004, the NFL donated $250,000 to the United Service Organizations to build a USO center in memory of Tillman. The Pat Tillman USO Center, the first USO center in Afghanistan, opened on Bagram Air Base on April 1, 2005.

In 2005, Mike Ricci of the Phoenix Coyotes switched his uniform number to 40 in honor of Tillman.

Forward Operating Base Tillman is close to the Pakistan border, near the village of Lwara in Paktika Province, Afghanistan.

On Saturday, April 15, 2006, more than 10,000 participants turned out for Pat's Run in Tempe, Arizona. The racers traveled along the 4.2-mile (6.8 km) course around Tempe Town Lake to the finish line, on the 42-yard (38 m) line of Sun Devil Stadium. A second race took place in San Jose.

Sponsored by the Pat Tillman Foundation, a total of 14,000 runners took part. In 2005, about 6,000 took part in a single race in Tempe.

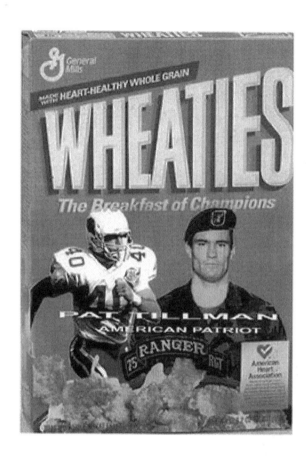

Just south of San Jose, California, in the small community of New Almaden where Pat Tillman grew up, a memorial was constructed near the Almaden Quicksilver County Park. This memorial was dedicated in September 2007 during the annual New Almaden Day celebration.

The skateboarding bulldog featured on YouTube and in an Apple iPhone commercial was named after Tillman.

Following Tillman's death, the Ohio State Linebackers Corp consisting of A.J. Hawk, Bobby Carpenter, and Anthony Schlegel, as well as center Nick Mangold grew their hair in tribute to Tillman, imitating Tillman's trademark locks.

In September 2008, Rory Fanning, a fellow Army Ranger who was stationed with Tillman in Fort Lewis, WA, began his "Walk for Pat" — a walk across the United States in an effort to raise money and awareness for the Pat Tillman Foundation.

Sources

"About Pat Tillman." *Pat Tillman Foundation*, http://www.pattillmanfoundation.org

"Boots on the Ground by Dusk: My Tribute to Pat Tillman." *Mary Tillman,* 2008.

"Marching to His Own Ideals." Melissa Isaacson, *The Chicago Tribune*, June 2, 2002.

"Misleading Information from the Battlefield: The Tillman and Lynch Episodes." United States House of Representatives Committee on Oversight and Government Reform, July 17, 2008.

"One of a Kind." *People,* May 10, 2004, Volume 61, No. 18, pp. 66-69.

"Pat Tillman." *Wikipedia, The Free Encyclopedia.*

"Where Men Find Glory: The Odyssey of Pat Tillman." *Jon Krakauer,* 2009.

Made in the USA
Lexington, KY
14 December 2012